This Books Belongs To.........

....

....

....

Trace the steps for making the letter a on the following line.

$\overline{}$
$i \quad i \quad a \quad a \quad a \quad a \quad aa$

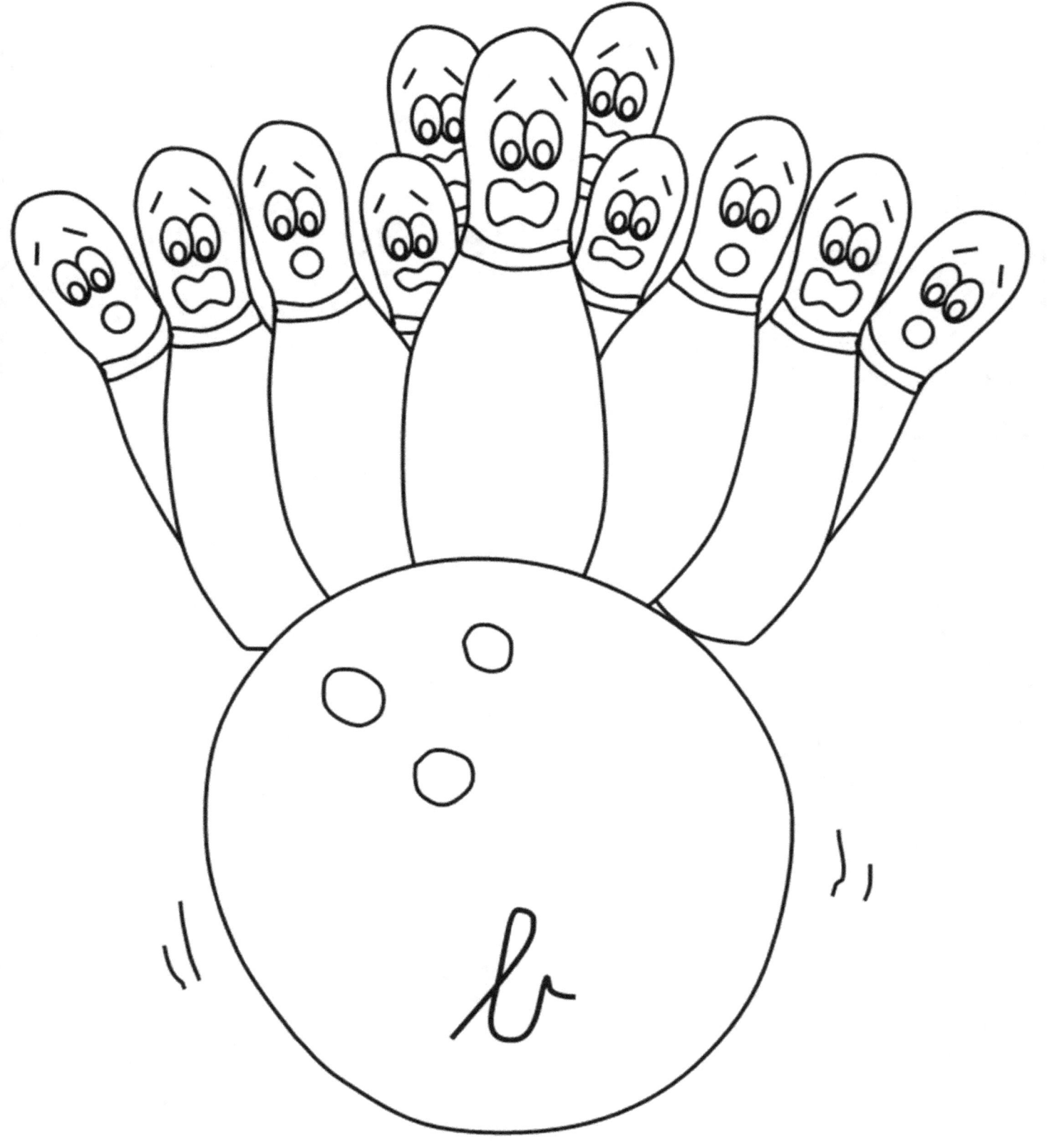

Trace the steps for making the letter b on the following line.

Trace the steps for making the letter c on the following line.

Trace the steps for making the letter c on the following line.

c   h   ch   ch   ch   ch

Trace the steps for making the letter d on the following line.

_ _
 d   d   d   d   d   dd

Trace the steps for making the letter e on the following line.

Trace the steps for making the letter f on the following line.

Trace the steps for making the letter g on the following line.

Trace the steps for making the letter h on the following line.

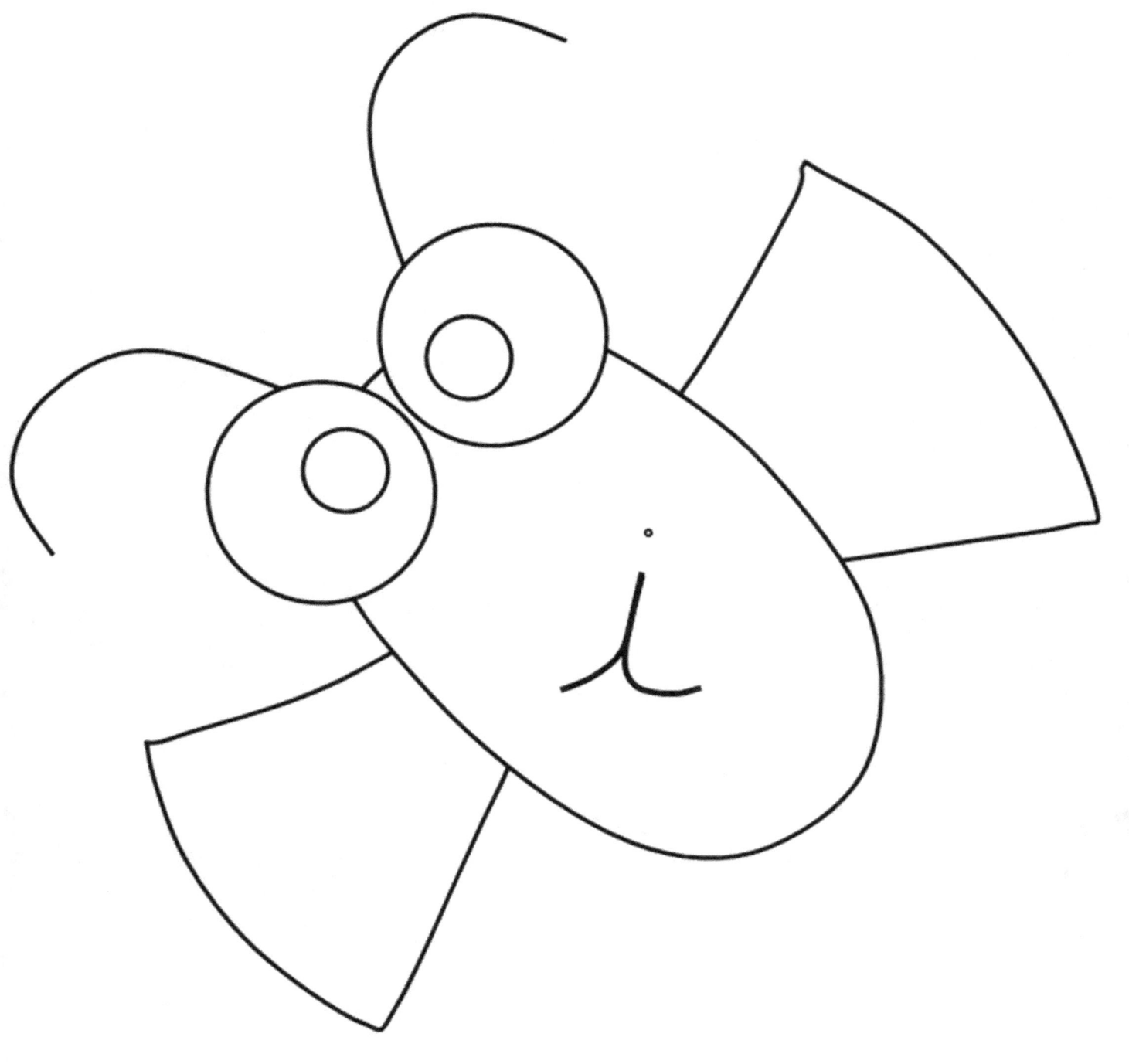

Trace the steps for making the letter i on the following line.

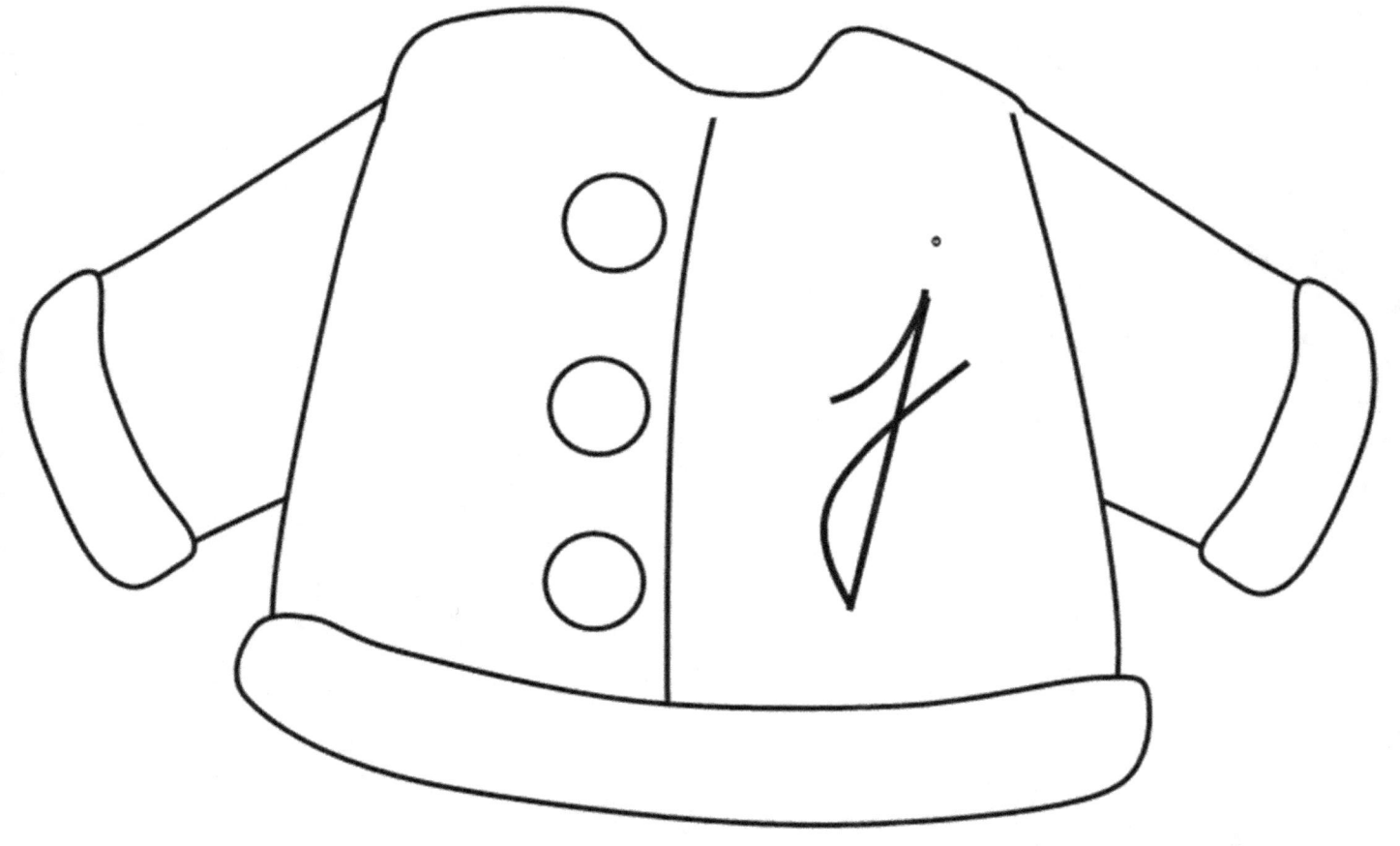

Trace the steps for making the letter j on the following line.

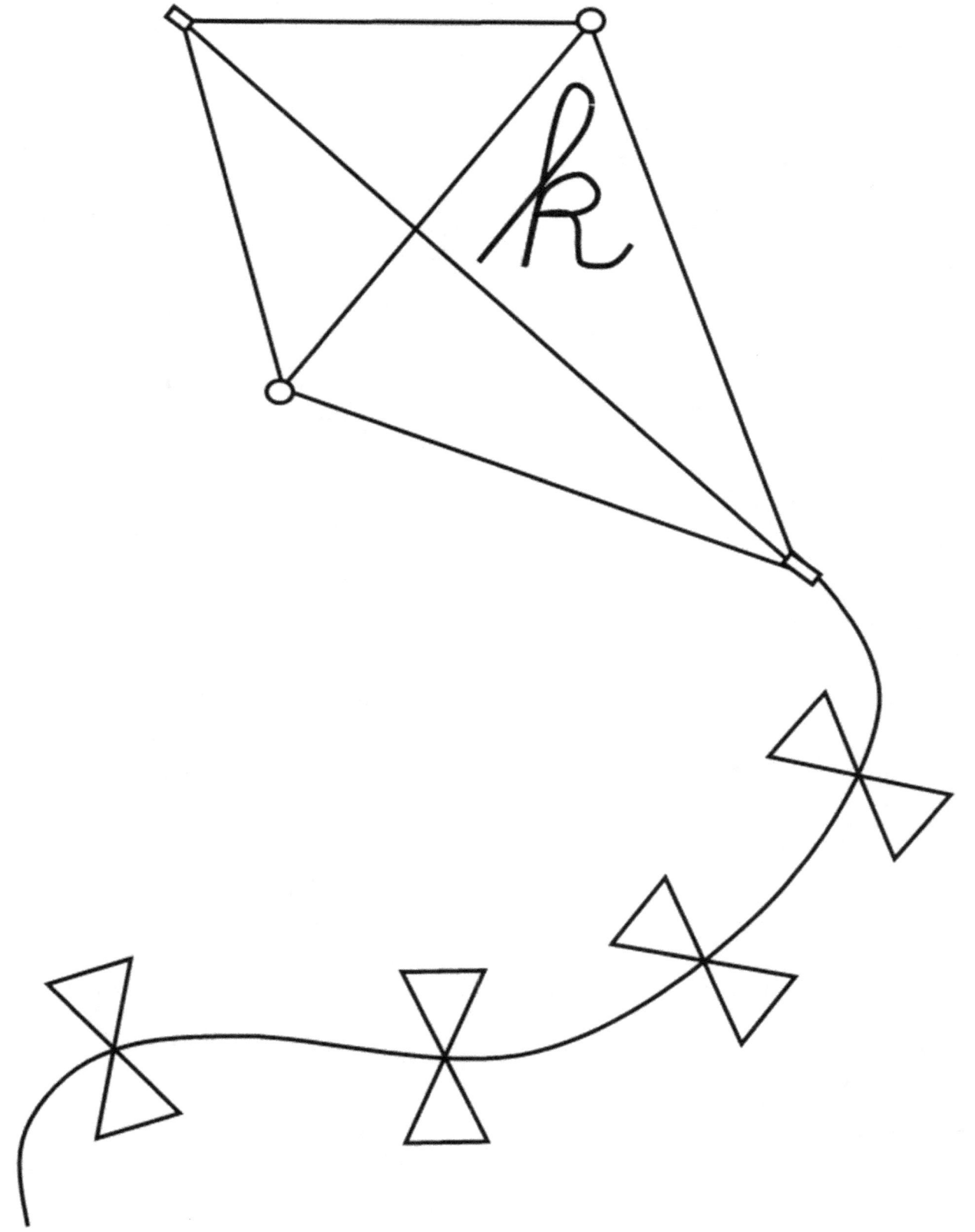

Trace the steps for making the letter k on the following line.

Trace the steps for making the letter l on the following line.

Trace the steps for making the letter m on the following line.

_____

ⅉ ⅉ 𝓂 𝓂 𝓂 𝓂 𝓂 𝓂 𝓂 𝓂

Trace the steps for making the letter n on the following line.

$n \quad n \quad n \quad n \quad n \quad n \quad n \quad nn$

Trace the steps for making the letter o on the following line.

Trace the steps for making the letter p on the following line.

p p p p p pp

Trace the steps for making the letter q on the following line.

r r a q q q q

Trace the steps for making the letter r on the following line.

Trace the steps for making the letter s on the following line.

Trace the steps for making the letter sh on the following line.

s h sh sh sh

Trace the steps for making the letter t on the following line.

Trace the steps for making the letter th on the following line.

t *h* *th* *th* *th* *th*

Trace the steps for making the letter u on the following line.

_____

U U U U U U U U U U U UUU

Trace the steps for making the letter v on the following line.

Trace the steps for making the letter w on the following line.

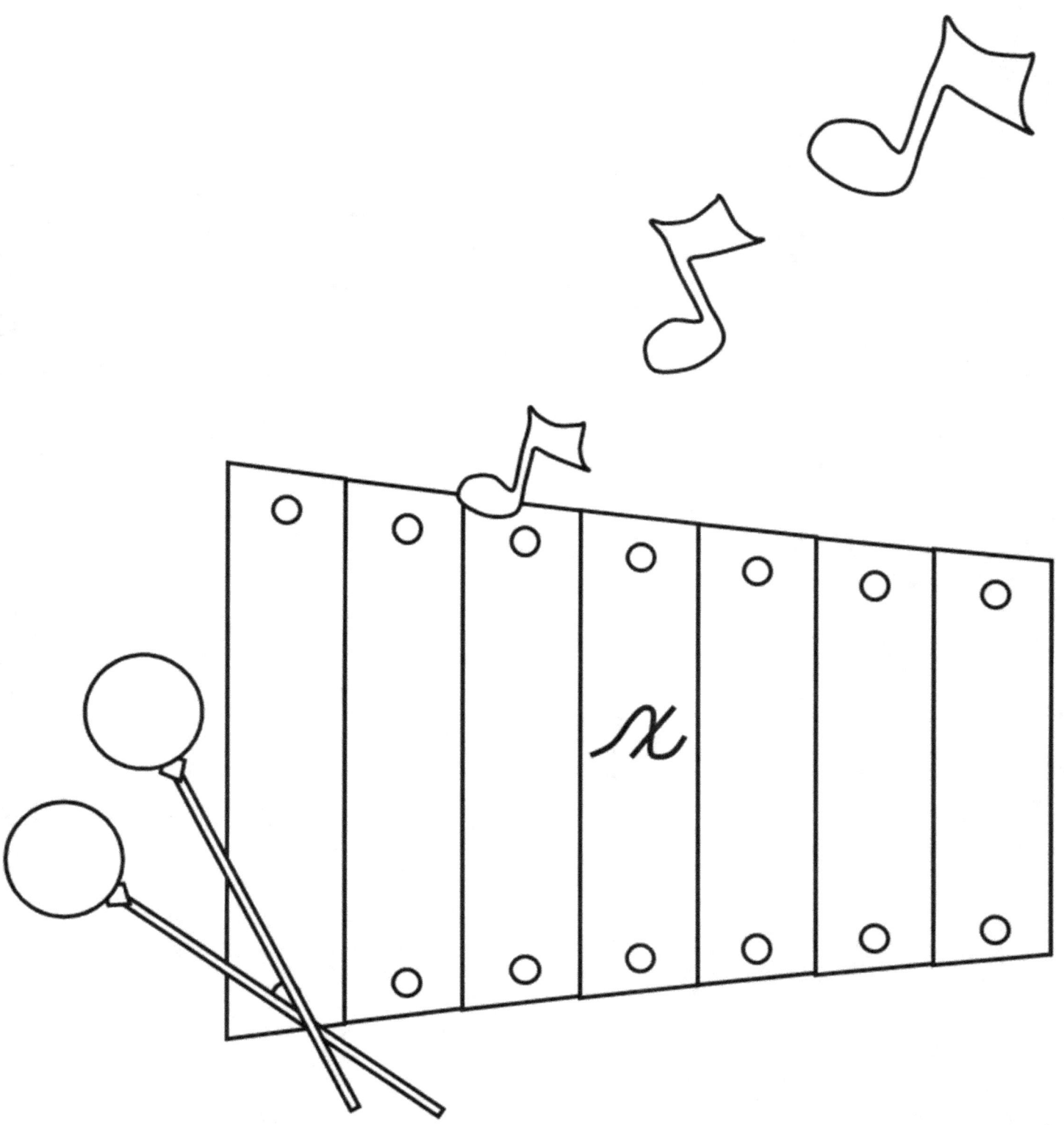

Trace the steps for making the letter x on the following line.

Trace the steps for making the letter y on the following line.

Trace the steps for making the letter z on the following line.

www.ingramcontent.com/pod-product-compliance
Lightning Source LLC
Chambersburg PA
CBHW081512220526
45467CB00010B/2880